TULLY GOES ON HOLIDAY

Available in the Tales of Tully series

Tully's Life
This heart-warming story follows the journey of Tully from street dog to much-loved family pet, teaching young readers about the importance of kindness, understanding and hope.

Tully Takes Off!
Tully has arrived in her new home with her new grown-up, but she does not like it one bit! When Tully sees an opportunity to go back to her old life on the streets - the only life she has known up to now - she takes it with both paws. With a search underway, it is up to her new grown-up to work out what Tully needs and help get her safely home.

Tully and the Sad Day
Tully has woken up feeling grey and cloudy inside and she does not know what to do. She cannot help her big feeling because she does not know what it is. As her different feelings begin to work together in the wrong way, it is up to Tully's grown-up to help her to understand what she needs.

Go To Sleep Tully!
It is night time and Tully is tired, but she does not want to go to sleep. Her new grown-up knows that Tully is trying every trick she can to avoid going go to bed! With lots of adventures planned and Tully needing her rest, Tully's grown-up needs to find a way to help Tully learn to not be so worried about bedtime.

Tully and the Midnight Feast
Tully is a newly-adopted dog settling in with her new grown-up. Since her arrival, her snacks have started mysteriously disappearing from the cupboard and appearing under her bed, she seems to have forgotten her manners, and there are days when she just cannot stop eating! Tully and her grown-up need to work together to help Tully with her worries about food.

Tully and the Scary Day
Tully has woken up feeling scared. She isn't really sure why, but today feels like a very scary day, and she just wants to hide. Tully's grown-up is thankfully there to help Tully manage her big feelings and see that the day is not so scary after all.

Don't Touch Tully!
Tully is settling in with her new grown-up. She has learned that the new grown-up is a safe person and she enjoys strokes and cuddles with them. Then Tully starts to meet new people, who want to show her how loved she is. Unfortunately, Tully doesn't feel the same about people she does not know and trust. It is up to Tully's grown-up to find a way to help Tully with her big feelings and to be Tully's voice, when she can't use hers.

Tully and the Tummy Ache
Tully has a tummy ache and it's making her feel quite grumpy. She doesn't want to eat or drink, and she can't get comfortable. Her tummy is sore and it's getting worse! Tully is in a toilet muddle. So, Tully and her grown-up work together to sort the muddle out and help Tully to cure her tummy ache.

Tully's Birthday
It's Tully's birthday, and her grown-up has planned a special day for her, but Tully doesn't feel like celebrating. As the day begins to unfold, so do Tully's big feelings. Tully doesn't know what to do about the big feelings, so she does a bad thing. Luckily, Tully's grown-up is there to help her feel better about herself, and enjoy the rest of her birthday.

Listen, Tully!
Tully does not always like to listen, especially when her grown-up is trying to stop her having fun. Tully decides that instead of listening, she can be in charge. But when things start to go wrong, Tully and her grown-up need to work out how Tully can begin to find listening a little bit easier.

Tully and the Makeover
Tully has been having lots of fun playing in the mud, but now her grown-up says she has to have a bath. Oh dear! Tully is not sure she wants one of those. She is feeling a bit nervous about what is going to happen to her, but Tully's grown-up shows her that there is nothing to worry about. Having a bath is a good thing after all.

Tully and Vera
Tully has moved in with her new grown-up but she is missing her foster carer, Vera. Tully is struggling to understand why she had to leave, and whether it is okay to have big feelings about Vera. It is up to Tully's grown-up to try and help her to understand loss and endings and why, sometimes, they have to happen to make space for new beginnings.

Tully and the Chase
Tully loves to be chased. It gives her a feeling of excitement which starts off as being fun, but one day the excited feeling suddenly and very quickly becomes a feeling which is too big. Instead of feeling excited, Tully starts to feel scared. Tully and her grown-up need to work out how they can play Tully's exciting game without it becoming a bit too much for her, and causing a muddle.

Tully at Christmas
Things are starting to feel a bit different in Tully's house and all around outside. Tully's grown-up looks different, strange lights are appearing everywhere and people have started putting their gardens indoors! Tully is not sure what to make of this thing called Christmas – she just wants everything to stay the same. What can Tully's grown-up do to make Christmas-time a nicer time for both of them?

Tully Goes on Holiday
Tully has gone on a holiday with her grown-up. After a difficult start, things seem to be going well. But when the fairground opens up, with all its flashing lights, loud music and food smells, Tully's big feelings get the better of her, making her want to run. And she does! Tully's grown-up needs to find her in time to show her that holidays can be fun after all.

Tully and the New Rules
Tully likes lots of things about living in a house with her grown-up, but one thing she really doesn't like is all the rules! Tully thinks the rules are all very boring and her grown-up must want to stop her from having fun. One day Tully breaks her least favourite rule, and something bad happens. Tully doesn't know what to do! Can Tully's grown-up get to the bottom of this muddle so it doesn't happen again?

Tully Goes on Holiday

TALES OF TULLY

Jess van der Hoech

Trauma Tools & Training

Acknowledgements

As always, to my trusted editor Sarah Ogden for all that you do to make these books come to life. I will never fully know what goes on behind the scenes, but it is a joy to work alongside you on these projects. Thank you.

Thank you to my supervisor Linda Hoggan for your continued support, encouragement, discussion and much-welcomed feedback on this series. I learn so much from you and the knowledge I have gained form our conversations has been invaluable across my practice, the books and now this series. Thank you.

Thank you to Laura Benham, for your support in giving me feedback, the searching questions, your friendship and of course, the countless conversations about dogs, the content of which has become quite useful! Thank you.

To the children and families who I meet in my therapy room, from whom I have learned more about hope and healing than any course could ever teach me. Your input, ideas, questions and answers are so valuable to me and I will be forever grateful. Thank you.

Preface

The *Tales of Tully* series is based on the adoption of an ex street dog from Bosnia who came to live with me in September 2023. Watching her try to settle and adapt from everything she had previously known to fit in with a new way of life began to present a number of ideas as to how to communicate such difficulties that can be experienced, to others who are in the process of adopting or who have adopted children. The aim of the series is to provide an opportunity to explore different situations, circumstances, feelings and experiences, finding new ways of communicating and understanding each other, through the voice of Tully.

Going on holiday can be an experience that many families look forward to. It can often be an exciting time, but plane journeys, car journeys, new experiences, new beds to sleep in, different sights, sounds, smells, foods and so on, are all things that a child who has experienced developmental trauma may struggle with. The holiday that has been worked hard for and saved up for, anticipating that it will be well-received and appreciated, can become a very highly charged and difficult experience.

Sometimes, adults might assume that their children would love to go on a big holiday; a huge theme park with lots of dressed-up characters, rides, music and parades – you know the kind! But often, this is not the ideal holiday, simply because there is too much stimuli. The ideal holiday might actually be camping in the woods; back to basics, particularly in the early days of a new adoption.

I have worked with some families who holiday in the same place every year, the same location, even the same accommodation, so the child knows exactly what to expect. While this may seem boring to some, it does significantly reduce the level of overwhelm both on and leading up to the holiday. Aside from the first visit, there will be answers to questions that the child might have which can reduce anxiety.

If the holiday is going to be to a new place, doing lots of research first, getting photos, ideas of what is on in the area and what you might be doing will help to plan and give the child a level of understanding as to where and what the holiday will entail.

I have not yet tried to take Tully on a holiday because she is so exceptionally nervous, the closest we have got to such a new experience was when I took her to my new office. She was already dysregulated from the car journey which she did not like, and the first thing she did when we got into the room was to try and jump out of the window, presumably so she could go on the run again!

I stayed with her, quietly alongside her as she began to settle. I had taken her high value reward treats with me, but at first she would not be bribed! After a while, she did begin to calm down and even had a snooze in her dog bed which I had left there the day before, so she could smell something of hers as soon as she arrived.

The more we go somewhere new and then come back home, the more she is starting to learn that we can go and do new things and have new experiences and she is safe. It is something that I have put on repeat, we do the same things over and over and over again. This is how ultimately she will begin to learn, not only about the new experiences she is having, but that she can trust me to keep her safe wherever it is we might be.

This same theory needs to be applied to children who have experienced developmental trauma; they need to trust that they can be kept safe in a different place as well as at home.

This book has been written to help children and their grown-ups to explore some of the big feelings that may come about in relation to going on holiday.

How to use this book

First and foremost, ensure that both you and the child are well-regulated and comfortable when you begin to read Tully's story. Make sure you choose a time when you are unlikely to be interrupted. The child may like a soother, a favourite or fidget toy, a drink or something to suck or chew to help them to stay regulated.

If the child is calm, then begins to try and distract or move away from the reading, make a note of what they have just heard in the text. It is very likely that they will have just provided you with some valuable information about something that they cannot tolerate or want to avoid for now.

The questions have been designed not only to explore the internal world of the child, but to help to develop a common language between the child and adult who are using this book together. The child cannot get the answers to the questions incorrect. Their interpretation of the thoughts and feelings Tully is having may provide some very significant information about the child's own thoughts and feelings. The child may want to expand the answers to talk about themselves and may even be able to make comparisons between Tully's feelings and their own.

Tully Goes on Holiday

It was a sunny day and Tully was resting after her delicious breakfast.

"Come on Tully, it's time to go!" her grown-up said. "We're going on holiday!"

Tully noticed a big suitcase in the hallway. Her grown-up had a bag of Tully's things – her harness, favourite toys and some snacks. Tully was not sure about this at all.

Why might Tully be unsure of what is happening?

Tully and her grown-up got into the car. Usually Tully enjoyed a short car journey, but this one went on…and on…and on…and on.

How might Tully feel about driving so far away?

What worries might Tully have about the long car journey?

Eventually, Tully and her grown-up got out of the car and went into a new house. The grown-up started to look around.

"What am I doing here?" thought Tully. "I don't want to live here!"

Tully tried to run away, but the door was shut. Tully scratched at it to let her grown-up know that she wanted to leave.

What might Tully be thinking?

How might she be feeling?

"It's okay Tully" the grown-up said. "We are on holiday. We will stay here for a week and then we will go home again."

Tully wondered why they would move house for a week and then go home again. Tully did not understand what the point of this thing called a holiday was.

What are the good things about a holiday?

What are the bad things about a holiday?

Tully's grown-up brought her blanket from the car. There was a new bed for Tully to sleep in. The bed was very comfortable, but Tully did not lie in it for long. She wanted to let the grown-up know that she was not happy about this at all!

Why might Tully be being difficult?

The next day, Tully's grown-up took her to a place called 'the beach'. Tully had never been to a beach before. She loved it. It was early morning, and it was quiet and peaceful. Tully liked the feeling of the sand underneath her paws. She liked it when the waves came onto the sand and chased her! Tully played a game with the sea where it had to try and catch her and not wet her paws! Tully was having a lovely time.

What are the good things about the beach?

How is Tully feeling about the beach?

Tully had been having such a good time that she didn't notice it happening at first. More and more people were coming to the beach. Then a funfair opened up with lots of music playing. Food was being cooked at lots of different restaurants. All of the things to smell, hear and see all at once became too much for Tully. It made her want to run.

So she did.

Was this a good plan?

How might Tully have been feeling?

Tully ran to a quiet street away from the beach and hid under a car. As she began to calm down, she realised what she had done. She had run away and now she was lost and alone.

How might Tully be feeling now?

How might Tully's grown-up be feeling now?

It seemed like a long time before Tully heard her grown-up's voice calling her. She didn't want to be in trouble, but she didn't want to be alone any more either. Tully came out from her hiding place.

"Oh Tully! There you are!" her grown-up said. "You mustn't run off, I was worried about you!"

Tully felt bad. She did not want her grown-up to worry.

"Tully, I noticed that when it was quiet on the beach you enjoyed it. You didn't like it when it became too busy and noisy. We had a big change coming to stay in the new house and we should have stayed in there today and got used to it together before we came to the beach."

Would this have been a good plan?

Is there anything else that could help Tully?

"We won't come to the beach when it is so busy and noisy. I will find some quieter things for us to do and places that we can explore together that won't give you so many big feelings."

What kind of things might Tully like to do?

What kind of things would you like to do on a holiday?

The next few days were much quieter, just as her grown-up had promised. They found some quieter beaches to explore and some nice walks away from the crowds of people. They even found a special place for Tully to have a doggy ice cream.

Tully enjoyed spending time with her grown-up and by the end of the week, she was a bit sad to leave. But she was really happy to get home again!

About the author

Jess van der Hoech is a qualified therapist who has spent the last ten years studying and working with the impact of developmental trauma and, in particular, the assessment and treatment of children and adolescents with complex trauma and dissociation.

As well as supporting birth families, Jess works with looked-after and adopted children and families, using skills in attachment-focused therapy and therapeutic parenting techniques.

Jess is a supervisor, trainer and motivational speaker with a passion for writing therapeutic books that are accessible to children and families to help with the healing process and to increase awareness in the impact of trauma.

Also by Jess van der Hoech

What A Muddle (2016) ISBN 978 18381987 0 1 (Co-authored with Renée Potgieter Marks)
An interactive, practical workbook designed to help children who have difficulties with emotional regulation to begin to understand what is happening in their bodies. A variety of activities throughout the book enable the child to start to explore these ideas through the story of Sam, while gently encouraging them to begin to verbalise their own experiences. Carrying out the physical exercises in the book can promote changes in emotional regulation. The text is written in a child-friendly, gender-neutral style, and is easy to understand for parents, carers and practitioners alike. For children aged 4-12.

These Three Words (2018) ISBN 978 18381987 5 6
Also available as an e-book. A unique therapeutic novel for teenagers with the aim of linking together the feelings, emotions and behaviours connected to anxiety, with some of the therapeutic tools that can be used in order to enable better self-regulation, increased confidence and different ways of thinking. The book is equally valuable to parents of teenagers with anxiety, giving them an insight and understanding into some of the issues that may be affecting their child, and potentially opening up a line of communication and a way forward between parent and teen.

These Three Words: The Journal (2019) ISBN 978 18381987 2 5
A thought-provoking and hands-on workbook, combining a series of practical exercises and tools designed to assist teenagers who are struggling with the symptoms of anxiety. Addressing the anxious responses in both brain and body, this journal provides the reader with the opportunity to discover therapeutic coping techniques and learn how to apply them to their own personal problem areas, before committing to a twenty-eight-day practice to promote good emotional regulation and reduced anxiety. The journal can be used alongside the therapeutic novel These Three Words, or as a standalone workbook, and it is suitable for use by the teenage reader on their own, with a parent, or in a group.

Beastie, Baby and the Brand-New Mummy (2022) ISBN 978 18381987 3 2 and *Beastie, Baby and the Brand-New Daddy (2022) ISBN 978 18381987 4 9*
A therapeutic story that looks at the external signs of pathological dissociation in a child. Dolly's story helps children who have experienced early trauma to begin to understand, in a very simple way, what dissociation is and why it has happened in their internal world. Tools and techniques are included within the story that parents and caregivers can use to assist the child in the first stages of their healing process. Beautiful illustrations on every page enhance the story of Dolly, and help the reader to relate to the events that happen, to notice the methods Dolly has developed to manage her feelings, and to think about what is happening in their own internal world. For children aged 4-12

Printed in Great Britain
by Amazon

62815848R00025